STANLEY SANDLOT BASEBALL TEAMS

And the Road to Cooperstown

A True Story
by

Jennings Painter
with Donnie Wilson

Cover Design by Patrick Burns
Edited and Formatted by Marley Gibson
Project Coordinated by Sheila Jenkins

Any Internet references contained in the work are current at publication time, but Jennings Painter and Donnie Wilson cannot guarantee that a specific location will continue to be maintained.

Jennings Painter and Donnie Wilson
Stanley, Virginia

Printed in the United States of America

Published by Cardinal Rules Press

Cardinal Rules
———— PRESS ————

DEDICATION

This book is dedicated to the parents and grandparents of all the players acknowledging them for their support and encouragement and for teaching us to respect everyone. For their efforts, we are eternally grateful.

TABLE OF CONTENTS

INTRODUCTION...I

LET'S PLAY BALL...3

REMINISCING...12

IN THE WORDS OF DONNIE WILSON...21

ON THE ROAD TO "FAME"..27

THE TEAMS...36

ACKNOWLEDGEMENTS..37

ABOUT THE AUTHORS..39

INTRODUCTION

This is a true story about a bunch of kids who liked to play baseball and their amazing journey which led them to have their names and records entered into the Baseball Hall of Fame in Cooperstown, New York some sixty years later.

LET'S PLAY BALL

Located approximately one hundred miles from the nation's capital and the former Washington Senators' Griffith Stadium, a small town named Stanley, Virginia, provided an oasis of nature surrounded by rolling hills and mountains, quiet hollows, rushing streams and waterfalls, and deep green pastures.

As a young man growing up in this remote area, I often wondered what life would be like beyond the mountains of the Blue Ridge and the Appalachian. Life was simple and the friendships forged were the kind of relationships that last a lifetime.

Friendships fostered through the game of baseball.

In the 1940s and 1950s, baseball was about the only pastime for kids to play and enjoy. My favorite team was the Washington Senators and I idolized Mickey Vernon. He threw and batted left-handed. He was an American League All-Star for five of the ten years that comprised the decade of the 50s; two of those years being 1955 and 1956.

My brothers, friends, and I all wanted to emulate the big leaguers. My dad, Dickie, and my mom, Charlotte, fostered our love of the game and allowed us to play baseball when our chores were complete.

Another group of kids who loved to play were the children of Floyd Nauman. On Saturday and Sunday afternoons, there was usually a backyard ballgame at one of the family homes. Sometimes, even our parents and grandparents would join in the games. As these games became a ritual over the years, other kids in the neighborhood came and joined us.

As the children grew older and stronger, and the number of players increased, the backyard was no longer big enough to host the games. In 1953, play was moved to a cow pasture behind the home of Ray and Dorothy Sours. Then, in 1954, the games were moved, yet again, to another cow pasture behind the home of Floyd and Beulah Nauman. We always had the newer and younger players check for any "hot" cow pies on the fields and find ways to clear or flag the obstacles. Because we didn't have money to buy equipment, we would use the dried cow pies as our bases.

America loved baseball and the residents of Stanley were no different. Several fields throughout town were utilized as ball parks, including the property of the Robert and Clarine Painter family, our first cousins. Many other kids from their neighborhood had started playing with them, also. The Floyd Nauman field was about a mile and a half from the Robert Painter field. After some serious negotiations between the kids, it was decided to formulate teams comprised of the two groups and play games on the same field. Some competitions were played on the Floyd Nauman field and some on the Robert Painter field.

One of my most vivid memories from the 1954 season includes the injury to Jerry Painter.

There was a barbed wire fence around the Floyd Nauman field that ran parallel from the first base line out to the right field corner. The fence was about three feet from the foul line and about ten feet from first base. On the home plate side, there was a broken strand of barbed wire with the end of it extending in toward the foul line.

In one game, Jerry hit a fly ball to left center field and was watching the outfielder as he ran toward first base. He got out of the baseline and caught his right arm in the barbed wire. We ran to find a doctor and many stitches were required to close the cut. Jerry still has scars even today.

Another memory involved the hog pen behind the left field fence. The pen was loaded with fleas, so if someone hit a ball over that way, you had to climb over the fence to retrieve the ball. The fleas were quick to invade and by the time you arrived home at night, you were covered with bites. We knew that meant much scolding from our parents in addition to a dousing in rubbing alcohol. To this day, I haven't determined which was worse, the talking to or the bites.

My favorite memory from 1954 is from one of the games where my team was leading by one run with two outs in the bottom of the last inning. Our left fielder was Margie Nauman, a girl who was just as good as the boys. The home team had runners on second and third. The batter hit an easy fly ball to the left field, but the usually sure-handed Margie dropped the ball. Two runners scored and we lost the game.

Back then, every player had a nickname. Margie was real skinny and lean, so we called her "Lena." As we gathered around home plate after the game, some of my teammates began telling Lena it was her fault we lost.

I was upset, so I also chimed in. "Yes, 'Lena the Hyena' lost the game for us."

She didn't say anything, but gave me a hard stare.

We all left the field with our heads hanging low.

A few days later, I was in my backyard. Lena's house was within shouting distance of ours and I heard someone calling from the front yard.

Lena called my name twice, "Hey J. C. Hey J. C."

I answered, "What do you want?"

She replied, "Can't I call my dog without you answering?" She was paying me back for calling her "Lena the Hyena."

There are so many wonderful memories from those years playing in the cow pastures. My grandfather, Cletus Painter, made a bat for me; one I attributed to my consistent ability to get on base. Also, we were very resourceful. We would get broken bats from the Stanley Town Team, nailing them back together and wrapping tape over the break.

Many of the kids didn't have gloves, so we would share. Uniforms were nonexistent. We wore bib overalls for three days before washing. After the garments were cleaned, we'd wear them another three days.

As the 1954 season ended, we were told we could not use the Floyd Nauman field anymore because we were wearing out the grass. There was also much debate about who had hit the most home runs, who was the best hitter, who was the best pitcher, and so forth.

Being a lover of statistics and Mickey Vernon's biggest fan, I closely monitored the performance and stats of the Washington Senators' first baseman. I was also a first baseman. I decided then that in 1955, I was going to find a way to document the results of everyone's performance playing in the cow pastures of Stanley, Virginia.

However, we still needed to find a new place to play.

In the spring of 1955, we received the good news that we could play on Donnie Wilson's property. This gave us two fields since the Robert Painter family allowed us to continue playing on their property. I also knew if I was going to keep stats and document data, we had to organize two teams who would have the same players for every game. It was decided the players from the Robert Painter area would be called the Shady Grove Dodgers and would play their home games on the Robert Painter field. The players from the Floyd Nauman area would be called the Piney Wood Tigers and would play their home games on the new Donnie Wilson field.

There was much excitement amongst the players on both teams knowing they would have a home field and a team name. Before the season started, I explained to everyone about keeping stats and told them each player was required to write down exactly what they did in every at bat. We operated on the honor system.

I told them to write small enough so we could get the information on one line because the next line was for the following batter. If a player got a hit and was left on base, he was required to record the information on his line before going out to the field. After each game, I took the sheets home and recorded the score and stats in one composition book.

The Piney Wood Tigers won the 1955 regular season with a record of 32 wins and 29 losses. The Shady Grove Dodgers had a record of 29 wins and 32 losses. The playoffs were discontinued with the two teams tied at two wins each. Since school had begun, the teams were not able to get enough players to finish the playoffs. That meant the 1955 championship was awarded to the regular season winner, the Piney Wood Tigers.

Some of my fondest memories of the season—other than playing—were walking down to the nearby county store and getting Topps Baseball cards with bubble gum included. We would put in a couple of big pieces of bubble gum and hold it in our jaw pretending to be just like the major league players who constantly had a big chew of tobacco in their mouth.

Another memory was having a big bucket of water with a dipper so both teams could get a drink when needed. We would put a towel over the bucket to keep the gnats and flies from diving in for a cool bath. This memory sticks with me to this day because we were young kids and had to learn to be resourceful in any way possible in order for us to play the game of ball we loved so much.

For 1955, the home run king was Nelson Painter with a total of eighty-six. I was awarded batting champ with an average of 713. Yes, it was an honor system.

The 1956 season began with the same two teams as the year before. The games that year were six innings each instead of nine. The Shady Grove Dodgers won the 1956 regular season with a record of 26 wins and 21 losses. The Piney Wood Tigers finished with a record of 21 wins and 26 losses. There were no playoffs, so, once again, the regular season winner took the championship title.

For 1956, the home run champion was Nelson Painter with thirty. I repeated as the batting champ with an average of 707.

It was an honor and thrill to record the statistics for all the players for the 1955 and 1956 seasons. These stats included the box scores for every game, at bats, hits, runs scored, and home runs. Also, the winning and losing pitchers for each game were documented. There were plans to play again in 1957, but as young boys do, we grew up. Fortunately,

I was talented enough—and now old enough—to play baseball with the Stanley Town Team.

Sadly, the Dodgers and the Tigers disbanded. However, there are remnants beyond the 1955 and 1956 teams no statistic could ever capture; friendships were forged and relationships continued that lasted throughout our lives.

As a member of the Stanley Sandlot Baseball Group, I am honored, once again, to embrace my teammates as we head to Cooperstown and fulfill a dream we all had standing in those pastures so many years ago – having our names and records entered into the Baseball Hall of Fame.

REMINISCING

In the weeks before our trip to the Baseball Hall of Fame in Cooperstown, New York, I had time to think back over those seasons and remember other things that happened to me. Also, I had discussions with some of the other players who relayed their tales to me.

Here are those stories and how our trip to Cooperstown all came about.

When I was ten years old, I got stuck under my grandfather, Cletus's, house. It was a frame house with a rock foundation that had a vent hole on the side where I would throw balls against it and let them bounce back to me. The vent hole was covered by a screen to keep pets from getting under the house. One day, I was throwing hard with a new ball I had just bought at a local store. On one of my throws, the ball broke through the screen and went under the house.

Being upset, I went through the vent hole and retrieved the ball. When I tried to get out, I could not get back through the hole. My brothers and sisters ran and got my grandmother, Esta, who brought grease for me to rub on myself, but I still could not get through the hole. We finally had to use a hammer and crow bar to remove the wooden frame around the vent hole and I was able to crawl out.

Another great memory was all the Painter family going to Uncle Mike and Aunt Ardith's farm on Sunday afternoons, having a big ball game, and then going for a swim in the "Blue Hole," a small lake formed in Naked Creek which ran through their properties. Our cousins, Alvin and Sylvia Painter, would lead us through the field to the Blue Hole. This is where we spent several hours with the adults in the family cooling off after the hot days of playing ball.

As kids, when we were playing ball, we never wanted to stop. On one occasion, it was getting close to supper time. My mother, Charlotte, sent word by my sister, Judy, for us to come eat now or we would not get any food. My mom was the best mother ever, but she knew our love for playing ball was so great that she had to threaten us with *no* food in order for us to stop playing and come home.

Once, we were playing a pickup game on the Floyd Nauman field. My sister, Jean, had to use the Nauman's outdoor toilet, and when she returned to the playing field, she went over and told the Nauman girls, Margie, Patsy, and Joyce, that they must be rich because their toilet had two seats. (Most toilets in those days only had one seat.) These memories don't necessarily pertain to the "game" of ball, but it helps set a picture of the time. No video games. No cell phones. No distractions that kept us molded to sofa cushions. Rather, we had days of sunshine, being outside, being together, and moving around playing to our heart's content which makes me smile as I look back at the simplicity of it all.

As I've said, about every kid had a nickname. Danny Nauman was small and skinny so we called him "Jake the Flake." Rondal Painter had a long scar down the middle of the top of his head, thus, we nicknamed him "Arch" after the Washington Senators' announcer, Arch McDonald whose parted hair resembled Rondal

On one occasion, Nelson Painter had not worn a shirt. It was a hot, clear day and we started playing ball around ten a.m. By one p.m., Nelson was getting quite sunburned. He kept running to the shade whenever he could, but two hours later, he was getting sick from the sunburn and heat. He had to go home where his mother, Clarine, soaked him with vinegar. Nelson didn't care. It was all part of the game.

The fun.

The challenge.

All that mattered, regardless of what circumstances or conditions came up, we were willing to endure *anything* for the love of playing ball.

One of the biggest arguments our teams ever had occurred during the 1954 season.

It was the bottom of the last inning in a pick-up game. The home team trailed by two runs and there were two outs. Roger Painter was the runner on third base and Johnny Painter was on second. Kenny Nauman hit a line drive over the center fielder's head. There were cows in the outfield and Roger Berry, who was playing center field, ran back after the ball.

Just when it looked like the ball was going to fall for a base hit, it slammed into a cow and popped up into the air. Roger was able to make the catch on the fly.

That was when the big argument took place:

"If the ball hadn't hit the cow, it couldn't have been caught!"

"Yeah, well the ball never hit the ground and should be an out!"

...and on and on it went.

The two sides never agreed and it was never settled. So, the game was called without the final score being settled.

During the 1955, season Roger Bradley—who lived in Luray, the next town seven or eight miles north of Stanley—rode his bike to the ball field. After the game, Roger discovered he had a flat tire. He was going to have a long walk home until Donnie Wilson loaned him his bike so he would not have to walk home.

Some players did not have bikes and would walk through the fields to the Robert Painter field. We had to be careful when climbing through the barbed wire fences so as not to tear our bib overalls or else we would get a good scolding when we got home. On our way through the fields, there was a well with a pump on our grandfather's property. We would always stop and get a good cold drink of water.

One of the biggest complaints about the Donnie Wilson field was when the ball got by the catcher, it would roll a long way because there was no backstop. That was, until someone came up with a great alternative.

Johnny Housden's father had an old, broken down 1935 Ford. Johnny used his father's tractor to pull the car over behind home plate and we used it as the backstop for the rest of the season.

Other memories from the 1956 season included the time Jerry Stillwell was playing left field for the Piney Wood Tigers and Danny Price hit a fly ball down the left field line that Jerry caught in foul ground. In making the catch, Jerry stepped into a fresh cow pile. He threw the ball back into the infield and decided to clean off his shoes while still in foul ground. The next Dodger batter was Danny Kaye Tobin and on the first pitch, he hit a line drive to left field. Jerry was still cleaning his shoe and the ball landed in for a double.

The next day, Jerry was traded from the Tigers to the Dodgers. He later remarked he didn't know if he was traded for stopping to clean his shoes or for some other reason.

In another game, Bruce Huffman hit a line drive to center field and Earl Kibler made a diving catch in between two cow piles. In another game on the Robert Painter field, William "Bread" Goode hit what looked like a sure home run over the fence in left center. Harvey "Duke" Painter jumped the four-foot-high fence and made a leaping catch. He fired the ball into second base to Junior Richards, the Tigers' second baseman. Junior caught the throw and stepped on second base doubling up Jimmy Painter who was on his way to third thinking the ball could not be caught. Out!

In another game, the Tigers' Kenny Purdham hit a ball over the left field fence. Stevie Painter, the Dodgers' left fielder, climbed through the fence to rob Kenny of a home run. This may not seem like a big deal, but it is a great memory as Stevie was small enough to slither quickly through the fence and make such an outstanding play. It left him with a great sense of pride as it did his teammates.

On one of our trips to the local country store to get bubble gum, Bucky Nauman decided he was going to try some real tobacco instead of merely chomping on gum. He put a big chew into his cheek and about fifteen minutes later, he got real sick and started throwing up. That'll show you trying to do grown up things when you're still growing up is not always a good idea. What seemed like a good idea at the time wasn't necessarily the best decision.

To this day, Bucky has not chewed any more tobacco.

One day, Willard Jenkins showed up to play and brought along his sister, Patsy. When Willard asked if she could join us, there was much grumbling by Francis and W.J. Huffman, Stevie Yates, and John Belton. At the time, when Lena played, we had not broken off into teams, so it was just whoever wanted to play at the time. Now, the stakes seemed a bit higher as we were now officially two teams. They did not think a girl was good enough to play with the boys on a "team," After some grumbling, they decided to let her play. In the first inning, she made a fine running catch of a line drive off the bat of Shirley Goode. When Patsy came to bat, we told our outfielders—Vincent "Cous" Housden, Dee Goode, and John Shepard—to play in close. We thought she would not be able to hit the ball very far. Patsy promptly knocked a line drive over all their heads scoring Alvin Painter, Ricky Robertson, and Gene Purdham. The relay from Ralph "Doodle" Harlow to Jerry Wilson, who was playing third base, was not in time and Patsy was safe with a stand-up triple. She got a whooping big cheer from everyone on the Dodgers' team.

We found out that day we could have not been more wrong about being hesitant when it came to letting Patsy play. She turned out to be a very valuable player.

I enlisted in the Army in 1958 along with one of my teammates and buddy, Shirley Goode. While I was in Germany in 1960, I was good enough to play baseball with Kaiserslautern of the United States Army league. On one occasion, we went to Amsterdam, Holland, for an exhibition game. There were young boys who came up and asked for our autographs. I wondered why they would want my autograph. I would never be in the Baseball Hall of Fame.

Maybe they knew something I didn't know...

One day, in the summer of 2013, I was going through an old Army trunk in my attic. I came across a composition book that contained the records and stats of the Piney Wood

Tigers and the Shady Grove Dodgers. These records were for the 1955 and 1956 seasons. I thought about who I should give the records to and decided they should go to my cousin, Jimmy Painter, who had also played for the Dodgers those years.

As things turned out, it proved to be a good decision.

IN THE WORDS OF DONNIE WILSON

In September 2014, I attended my wife's fiftieth reunion. Our first meeting with her class was at the new Page County High School for a tour of the school. I knew all of her classmates because I graduated a year before her.

We parked in the lot, walked into the school, and met a few of her classmates. When my wife went to greet her friends, I saw one of her classmates I knew from grade school and playing baseball within our area. I had not seen him for more than fifty years.

His name was Jimmy Painter.

I called him by name and shook his hand. He did not know me. I made the remark that he should feel bad not knowing me because I played ball with him when we were about ten years old. When my wife returned, he then knew who I was. We talked about our childhood and he asked me if

I knew his cousin, J.C. Painter, had recorded all the games we played? I expressed my interest in seeing the records.

About ten months later, I met another of the ball players I had not seen for a long time. I had lost contact with most all of my friends in Page County when I married and moved to Waynesboro, Virginia, in 1964. That player was Bucky Nauman who was my neighbor in the 1950s. We talked about the records J.C. had kept and passed on to Jimmy after finding them in his attic. Bucky said he had obtained a copy of the records and a few weeks later, I was given a copy.

There were many pages all hand written and detailed with dates of over a hundred games in 1955 and 1956.

I looked at the records on a regular basis for about ten more months. I couldn't believe J.C. had recorded all this information with names of players, scores, pitching records, batting averages, signing dates of new players, trades from one team to another, names of the two teams, and other information. I got the idea to get together with Jimmy, Bucky, Nelson Painter, manager of the Shady Grove Dodgers, and, of course, J.C., the manager of the Piney Wood Tigers and our record keeper.

We agreed to meet for breakfast at the Hawksbill Diner in Stanley, Virginia, where we all grew up together. The five of us met often and had a great time talking about the past. In

March 2016, at one of our meetings, I said this would make a great story and the five of us agreed.

I contacted the former sports writer for *The Page News and Courier*, a weekly newspaper in the county. Even though Bill Meade had retired from the paper, I thought he might be interested in this story. He referred me to the current (at the time) sports writer, Sean Labar. Regardless of his hesitation, Sean met with us and on April 7, 2016, and then he printed our story in the local paper.

From the very beginning of our meetings, I would ask questions trying to get all the information I could about each one of the players by only having their names from records. I received phone numbers, addresses, and names of ten players who had passed away. Then, I started a search for the remaining thirty. I made contact with twenty-three of them for a dinner reunion at the Lighthouse Gospel Church in Stanley with nineteen saying they'd attend. It wasn't easy trying to locate the members, but it was fun.

Here's what I discovered:

STEVIE YATES – I was a classmate of Stevie's sister who lived near Fredericksburg, Virginia, at Lake of the Woods. She gave me his phone number in Canyon Lake, Texas.

EARL KIBLER – Someone said he lived in Maryland, but could not make contact. Later, someone said he lived in Front Royal, Virginia. I found a number and called and got an answering service. I left my name and number and why I was calling. A week after our reunion, I received a call from Earl saying he was sorry he had not checked his answering service after being away for a while and had missed the dinner.

DANNY PRICE – I got Danny's number from his sister who lives in Page County. Danny lives in Kilmarnock, Virginia, and was very eager to attend our reunion.

DANNY KAYE TOBIN – Danny's name was in the records as Kaye Tobin and was signed to play ball the same day as Pat Jenkins. Pat was a girl. so I assumed Kaye was, as well. Little was remembered about Kaye. Jimmy said Kaye was the middle name and the first name was Danny. He thought he was visiting family in the neighborhood, but that was all. I entered his full name and approximate age in an online search and got a large list in return. I picked the first name in Virginia and called a business number listed. A man answered the phone. I told him my name and was looking for Danny Kaye Tobin, age seventy, who would have played ball in Stanley, Virginia, in the 1950s. To my surprise, he said, "You got him." He talked about some of the players he could remember. I asked him if he knew Danny Price and he said, "No." Later on in our talk, I went back to the conversation about Danny Price and asked Tobin, "Are you sure you don't know him because Price also lives in Kilmarnock?" Tobin wanted to know if he was a doctor and I told him Price was a retired cardiologist. Tobin knew a Dr. Charles Price who attended the same church. Price's full name was Charles Daniel even though we knew him as Danny. What a thrill to locate two players in the same town who didn't remember playing together as kids. Both attended the reunion and I could hardly wait to introduce them.

RICKY ROBERTSON – No one could remember him. He may have been visiting family in Stanley at the time of the records. I got some information from Bruce Huffman. After several weeks of phone calls, I finally made contact with Ricky's widow in Alabama. He had passed away about three years ago. Indeed, he would visit family in Stanley and, as a kid, he had lived in northern Virginia.

JOHN SHEPARD – Lived in Stanley his whole life, but was one of the hardest people to find. I found out he had a sister in the Stanley area. I kept looking for someone to help me find her. One morning at the diner, I asked about John and if they knew his sister. She lived a few hundred yards from the diner. I knocked at the door of a trailer and this woman said, "Hi, Donnie. Please come in." She remembered me from high school and was excited about her brother playing baseball.

These are merely some of the things that occurred when trying to find team members and family contacts. I feel fortunate to say I found every player or, at least, a family member of all forty people in the records.

Everyone involved would soon come to know in the following few months that all their names and records were going to be in the Baseball Hall of Fame in Cooperstown, New York.

ON THE ROAD TO "FAME"

I wondered what would happen to the records when we all were gone.

The five of us were at the diner when I asked J.C. and Jimmy, "What's the plan to preserve the records?"

It was between the two of them to decide because J.C. had kept the records and then passed them to Jimmy to hold on to.

Neither one knew.

"Maybe the library in Stanley or a place in the county could take them," I suggested.

They didn't know.

I said, "How about the Baseball Hall of Fame in New York?"

We all laughed when J.C. said, "I always wanted my name to be there."

I thought about it for a month or two and decided to call Cooperstown. Why not? The worst they could say was, "No."

I contacted Jim Gates, who is the librarian at the Baseball Hall of Fame. I told him briefly about what we had in our possession.

He said, "We have a lot of baseball things like that. Why don't you send me a few pages of what you have?"

"I can do that. When do you think I'll hear back from you?" I asked, trying not to get overly-excited about the possibility.

He said, "Once I get the copies, it'll be about thirty days."

This was on April 29, 2016, and the copies were mailed that very afternoon with a delivery date of Monday, May 2nd. I received a letter back on Saturday, May 7th (dated May 4th) saying Mr. Gates wanted the records and to wrap the items and mail them to him.

I couldn't believe this was going to happen. It was really going to happen. To us. A group of kids who were simply playing ball and having fun in a small town like Stanley. Our records and stats from those magical summers were going to be a permanent contribution to baseball history.

I called Mr. Gates back. "May we deliver the papers to you in person?"

He thought for a moment and then said ,"Yes, but the staff and I are going to have to plan it all through because we're quite busy."

We were ecstatic!

The trip started out with about seven or eight players and Mr. Gates was okay with that. Then, the story about our group making the trip to Cooperstown appeared in the county paper and our group quickly grew to twenty.

I relayed all of this to Mr. Gates who was thrilled over the news. "We'll have to move you to a different room for the transfer of records."

The next thing we knew, our story made WHSV TV 3 news in Harrisonburg, Virginia, and our group size grew to thirty-five, causing another change for Mr. Gates.

Finally, when it was all said and done, our group totaled over fifty. To accommodate everyone, we chartered a bus to take the majority of attendees while some people drove in and others flew. In total, there were about seventy people in attendance at the ceremony.

And, like that, we donated our records on July 12, 2016 to *The* Baseball Hall of Fame.

It was a great day for us! None of us could have predicted this, nor could we have foreseen that some meticulous scribbling and recording keeping in a composition notebook would mean so much to so many.

The follow-up newspaper articles in *The Page News and Courier* and the story by Bill Meade in the *Staunton News Leader* tells all about the welcome we received from the Hall of Fame, the mayor of Cooperstown, and Mr. Gates and staff.

We would like to take this opportunity to generously thank Mr. Randy Arrington, Publisher and General Manager of VA Weeklies – Odgen Newspapers of Virginia, LLC, for allowing us to reprint their newspaper articles pertaining to our story and our day at the Hall of Fame.

Thursday, April 7, 2016   **PAGE NEWS and COURIER**   Page C1

sportsNEWS

Sean Labar, sports editor: sports@pagenewspaper.com

Donnie Wilson, J.C. Painter, Jimmy Painter, Nelson Painter and Floyd "Bucky" Nauman were part of a group of friends that played sandlot baseball in Stanley in 1955. They are pictured above in front of the barn where they used to play on Aylor Grubbs Avenue.

Sean Labar/Page News and Courier

Shady Grove Dodgers

Nelson Painter
Jimmy Painter
Jerry Painter
Randal "Arch" Painter
Williard "Tad" Jenkins
William Goode
Roger Bradley
Gene Purdham
Roger Berry
Junior Richards

Piney Wood Tigers

J.C Painter
Harvey "Duke" Painter
Roger Painter
Floyd "Bucky" Nauman
Danny Price
Vincent Howsden
Johnny "Lippy" Painter
Donnie Wilson
Danny Nauman
Johnny Housden

1955 leaderboard

Top 5 batters	Home Runs
J.C. Painter (.713)	Nelson Painter (86)
Nelson Painter (.636)	J.C. Painter (80)
Duke Painter (.608)	Kenny Nauman (26)
Jerry Painter (.558)	William Goode (9)
Randal Painter (.448)	Duke Painter (9)

A field of dreams

Friends reunite to reminisce of their days playing sandlot baseball in Stanley

By Sean Labar
Staff Writer

A grassy field resting on the side of Aylor Grubbs Avenue in Stanley, sits empty, awaiting the World Series.

Kids from every nook of town are anxiously finishing their daily chores, while making sure the tires on their bicycles are packed with air.

Floyd "Bucky" Nauman rushes to get the cows milked so that his parents will let him play.

For this group of neighborhood children, August 29, 1955, has been marked on their calendars for months. It is the pinnacle of a 60-game season, and the final contest between the Shady Grove Dodgers and the Piney Wood Tigers.

While it isn't the actual October classic between the New York Yankees and the Brooklyn Dodgers of 1955, it holds just as much importance to these youngsters.

Unseasonably cold weather cancelled the makeshift championship that day, and the Tigers claimed the ultimate prize based on their winning percentage.

Nelson Painter led the way with 41 hits and four home runs in the four-game series, while J.C Painter followed up with 36 hits and a home run.

Sixty-one years later, five members of the Dodgers and the Tigers reunite in the back room of Hawksbill Diner in Stanley, less than two miles away from the fields they used to call home.

"This is the first time that we have all been together since 1955," Jimmy Painter matters from across the table.

Sandlot baseball was a staple in the 1950's throughout the United States. There were few organized youth league teams and no video games or fancy technology to divert kids' attention. Instead, there was a group of budding emulating legends like Ted Williams and Rocky Colavito, while using a rustic barn as a backstop.

Many people struggle to remember the details surrounding their sandlot games, especially the ones that occurred more than six decades ago. But that isn't the case for Stanley legends of the Dodgers and the Tigers.

After each and every game, J.C. Painter recorded statistics from that day. He jotted down everything from batting averages to pitching percentages. Those memories will never be forgotten.

"I always liked stats and numbers," J.C. Painter said. "Every night when I went home I wrote it all down. It was just something

to do as a kid."

Some members of the group knew that Painter had tracked each game, while others didn't. But now, as they all meet for breakfast for the first time since those seemingly never-ending summer days, details begin to emerge.

Like how on August 21, the Dodgers signed Kaye Tobin and resigned Pat Jenkins. Shirley Goode was dropped that same day.

Or how the Tigers had 32 wins in 1955, while the Dodgers had just 29. Each play was meticulously written down so that those games could be relived again and again.

For Donnie Wilson — who is now 71 and retired — playing baseball with the neighborhood kids was one of the fondest memories from his childhood.

"There were no computers and hardly any TVs," Wilson said. "A lot of pride went in to winning

those games. Some kids would cry when they lost. There was nothing else to do. This was our number one thing."

On a given afternoon, as many as 35 kids gathered to play under the gleaming Shenandoah sun. Age groups ranged from 5 to 18, but it wasn't uncommon for someone's dad to fill in if a team needed an extra player.

Instead of an actual baseball they played with a sponge ball with a cork center that was purchased for 15 cents at the local five and dime.

"The first couple games, you could crush that thing," Wilson said. "But it would start to get worn out the more that we played. We would have to use tape to keep it together."

At the beginning of each April, a new Major League Baseball season kicks off. Each time one of these men hears the crack of a bat, or smells the scent of freshly cut grass, they will be instantly taken back in time to Aylor Grubbs Avenue.

Because that's where it all began.

Photos in the article were taken by Milo Stewart, Jr. of the National Baseball Hall of Fame. The article was written by Sean Labar, Staff Writer, and was published by *Page News and Courier*, originally running on April 7, 2016.

Thursday, July 14, 2016   PAGE NEWS and COURIER   Page C1

sportsNEWS

Sean Labar, sports editor; sports@pagenewscourier.com

Milo Stewart Jr./National Baseball Hall of Fame

Above, members of the old sandlot league in Stanley pose Tuesday morning on the stage in the auditorium of the National Baseball Hall of Fame in Cooperstown, N.Y. At right, Jim Gates, Librarian for the Hall, accepts the 1955-56 record book for the Shady Grove Dodgers and the Piney Wood Tigers from the young man who penned it, Jennings Painter.

Long road to Cooperstown

Hall of Fame considers sandlot record book unique piece of Americana

By Sean Labar
Staff Writer

COOPERSTOWN, N.Y. — Jennings Painter took the stage inside the auditorium of the National Baseball Hall of Fame in Cooperstown, N.Y. brimming with emotion. Instead of chairs, the aisles were lined with bleachers. The walls were painted to make the room feel like a baseball grandstand.

His hands were trembling. Years began to settle in.

As a youngster 61 years ago, Painter didn't know his knack for note keeping would lead him — and 18 of his closest buddies — to the Mecca of baseball.

On Tuesday morning, representatives from the Hall of Fame held a ceremony to accept the records Painter kept during the 1955-56 sandlot sessions in Stanley. Each summer, the neighborhood boys spent their days in a field off Aylor Grubbs Avenue in Stanley. Their games were organized and competitive. And as the sun began to fade, Painter pulled out his notebook, jotting down the statistics from that day.

After the notes were removed from Painter's attic 61 years later, the idea came to fruition. Why not try to store these in the National Baseball Hall of Fame?

An initial letter was sent to Cooperstown, and the idea morphed into reality.

The Hall of Fame wanted the records.

The legacy of the Shady Grove Dodgers and Piney Wood Tigers will be preserved forever.

See HALL OF FAME Page C2

Photos in the article were taken by Milo Stewart, Jr. of the National Baseball Hall of Fame. The article was written by Sean Labar, Staff Writer, and was published by *Page News and Courier*, originally running on July 14, 2016.

C2 Thursday, July 14, 2016

Hall of Fame

Continued from Page C1

A simple stroll through the halls of Cooperstown is like Christmas Day for a baseball fan. A game-worn jersey of former Washington Nationals' pitcher Jordan Zimmermann glistens in the light of the case in the opening display. Around the corner, a picture of Ty Cobb cruising in a Chalmers automobile is plastered across a wall. Cobb edged Cleveland's Nap Lajoie for the 1910 AL batting crown. The car was his prize.

The museum is entrenched in artifacts surrounding America's pastime. But according to National Baseball Hall of Fame Library Director Jim Gates, there is little to commemorate the days of sandlot baseball.

"In the history of baseball, sandlot plays an incredible role," Gates said. "The reason this is so unique is because there was a kid, making this notebook while games were being played. And then he moved it. It's a contemporary piece of Americana, and we are very pleased to have it."

As the 18 players and their families boarded the bus headed home for the Shenandoah Valley, emotions were evident. Many of these men hadn't spoken since their childhood, and were reunited over the game of baseball. Tales of dodging cow pies on the field and hopes for building a Stanley baseball museum were the focal point of conversation.

"This has been the most incredible experience of my life," former player Donnie Wilson said. "I consider everyone on those teams to be my family."

As Painter exited the stage, his hands had stopped trembling. The tears on his face were replaced with a grin. His teammates stood by his side, knowing they will always be part of baseball history.

Former Stanley sandlot baseball player Donnie Wilson fights back his emotions after meeting National Baseball Hall of Fame director Jim Gates for the first time.

Sandlot player Jimmy Painter shares a moment with an onlooker as the Stanley sandlot team enters the National Baseball Hall of Fame in Cooperstown, N.Y.

Photos in the article were taken by Milo Stewart, Jr. of the National Baseball Hall of Fame. The article was written by Sean Labar, Staff Writer, and was published by *Page News and Courier*, originally running on July 14, 2016.

This is something that will always be a part of baseball history and something our families will have forever. They can visit any time. Baseball fans around the world can see our records and know of our love and dedication to this wonderful game.

The team members still meet on a regular basis and have a board of directors and membership of ballplayers. We conduct fundraisers with proceeds returned to the Page County community. We are working on becoming a non-profit organization.

Sadly, there were about twelve members who were unable to go to Cooperstown due to severe health reasons and one member pass away about two weeks after the trip.

~~~

I have found many people on this journey who I had forgotten about and several who I would never have known.

The field we played on was my home place which I sold in 1972. When looking for a charter bus for our trip, I contacted Richards Bus Lines in Luray, Virginia. The woman who answered, Mrs. Wallace, wanted to know the bus size, where we were going, and other general information. I told her our baseball story and where we played in the Stanley area.

"Are you familiar with the area?" I asked.

She said, "Yes! And, guess what?

"What?"

"I now own the property you played ball on," she said proudly. (The property has changed hands since 1972.)

If this story wasn't told, I most likely would not have met Mrs. Wallace. Such a unique coincidence. It seemed like everything had come full circle to round out this amazing journey.

I am thankful for every single person I have met, as we all are. Old friendships were rekindled and new friendships were forged. We had all gone on with our lives and established careers and families.

Some have already passed on, but they are not forgotten nor will those memories of a time when life was simple and our love for ball was greater than anything.

Our story will forever be preserved as a piece of baseball history that started in the cow fields in Stanley, Virginia and led us on the road to Cooperstown, New York, right into the Baseball Hall of Fame record books.

We are eternally grateful.

THE TEAMS

**Stanley Sandlot Baseball Teams 1955-1956
Records entered into the Baseball Hall of Fame
Cooperstown, New York
July 12, 2016**

SHADY GROVE DODGERS

Nelson Painter
Jimmy Painter
Jerry Painter
Randal "Arch" Painter
Willard "Tad" Jenkins
William "Bread" Goode
Roger Bradley
Gene Purdham
Roger Berry
Stevie Painter
Frances Huffman
Bruce Huffman
W.J. Huffman
Pat Jenkins
Alvin Painter
Danny Kaye Tobin
Jerry Stillwell
Steven Yates
John Belton
Ricky Robertson

PINEY WOOD TIGERS

J.C. Painter
Harvey "Duke" Painter
Roger Painter
Floyd "Bucky" Nauman
Danny Price
Vincent "Cous" Housden
Johnny "Lippy" Painter
Donnie Wilson
Danny "Jake Nauman
Junior Richards
Johnny Housden
Kenny Nauman
Ralph "Doodle" Harlow
Jerry Wilson
Shirley Goode
Dickie Painter
Kenny Purdham
Earl Kibler
Dee Goode
John Shepard

ACKNOWLEDGEMENTS

We would like to acknowledge all who have helped us with our baseball story:

All the baseball members

The Town of Stanley, Virginia

Page County Board of Supervisors

Mark Stroupe

Gary Breeden owner of D.R.'s Quick Stop

Lighthouse Gospel Church

Sean Labor and Bill Meade

Preston Knight

Shenandoah Valley Electric Cooperative

Page News and Courier

The Staunton News Leader

WHSV- TV 3

Andrew Clay

Larry Knight and the BBQ Chicken Crew

Danette Wilson – Facebook Page

Hawksbill Diner and Sheila Jenkins

All of those who made donations to the group

And, all of those who we have failed to mention

ABOUT THE AUTHORS

Jennings (J.C.) Painter was born in Stanley, Virginia. On January 24, 1964, he married Dolores Wilt. J.C. and Dolores have two children, daughter Monica of Stanley, and son, Kevin, and his wife, Teresa, also of Stanley. J.C. and Dolores currently reside in Stanley.

~~~

Donnie Ray Wilson was born March 2, 1945, in Stanley, Virginia. In July 1964, he married Danette Painter. They have three children: Todd D. Wilson of Springdale, Arkansas, Aimee L. Baker of Fredericksburg, Virginia, and Tim D. Wilson of Powhatan, Virginia. They are also the grandparents of four grandchildren. Donnie and Danette reside in Waynesboro, Virginia.

Made in the USA
Middletown, DE
16 February 2019